SWIMMING AND DIVING

A TRUE BOOK

by
Christin Ditchfield

Children's Press®
A Division of Grolier Publishing

New York London Hong Kong Sydney
Danbury, Connecticut

The start of a women's swimming event

Reading Consultant
Linda Cornwell
*Coordinator of School Quality
and Professional Improvement
Indiana State Teachers
Association*

Author's Dedication:
*For my grandmother,
Joan Devereux Ditchfield.
She was to swim for England in
the 1940 Olympic Games,
which were canceled because
of World War II.*

**Visit Children's Press® on the
Internet at:
http://publishing.grolier.com**

Library of Congress Cataloging-in-Publication Data

Ditchfield, Christin.
    Swimming and diving / by Christin Ditchfield.
        p.   cm. — (a true book)
    Includes bibliographical references (p.) and index.
    Summary: Discusses Olympic swimming and diving competitions,
describing the four basic swimming strokes and the three basic diving
positions.
    ISBN 0-516-21065-3 (lib. bdg.)   0-516-27030-3 (pbk.)
    1. Swimming Juvenile literature. 2. Diving Juvenile literature.
[1. Swimming. 2. Diving. 3. Olympics.] I. Title. II. Series.
GV837.6.D58 2000
797.2'4—dc21
                                                                99-28189
                                                                CIP
                                                                AC

GROLIER
PUBLISHING 1 2 3 4 5 6 7 8 9 0 R 09 08 07 06 05 04 03 02 01 00

Contents

Amy Van Dyken
in competition

Guts and Glory

One of the most exciting events of the 1996 Olympics took place at a pool. Swimming in her first Olympic final, Amy Van Dyken finished in fourth place. After the race, she climbed out of the pool and fell on the deck. She could hardly breathe. Her legs were cramping. Some people wondered: was Amy really tough enough to face the challenge of Olympic competition?

She hadn't always been a really good swimmer. The girls on her high-school swim team laughed at Amy because she was tall and awkward. She had asthma, an illness that made it hard for her to breathe during exercise. Sports didn't seem to be a good choice for Amy, but she loved swimming. Amy kept

Amy worked hard to make it to the Olympics.

practicing, hour after hour. She was determined to show every-one that she could succeed.

Amy Van Dyken celebrates a victory at the 1996 Olympics

Somehow, after that first race in the Atlanta Olympics, Amy Van Dyken found the strength to compete again— and again. In other races that same week, she won four gold medals! She made history by becoming the first American woman to win so many gold medals in a single Olympics.

Speed, skill, strength, and determination—Amy Van Dyken showed the world what swimming is all about.

Things Have Changed

Swimming is one of the oldest and most popular sports in the world. Greek and Roman soldiers swam to keep in good physical condition. Sailors learned to swim for safety. American Indians taught the Europeans their overhand stroke. And at the

Ancient Assyrian stone
tablet showing people
swimming (above) and
an underwater shot of
a modern-day men's
freestyle race (right)

first modern Olympics in
1896, swimming was one of
the main events.

Years ago, swimming competitions took place in lakes, rivers, or seas.

Years ago, swimming competitions were very different than they are today. Races took place in rivers and seas rather than in pools. Crowds of people gathered to watch from the shore. The courageous swimmers had to battle the weather as well as the waves. The water could be freezing cold! The winner was often the swimmer who lasted the longest—the one who didn't give up.

Today, swimming competitions take place in specially built pools. An Olympic-sized pool measures 164 feet (50 m) long. The water temperature is kept at 78 degrees Fahrenheit (25 degrees Celsius). For competitions, the pool is divided into

Today, swimming competitions take place in specially built pools.

rows, or lanes, to keep the athletes from swimming into each other.

Swimmers wear bathing suits made from special fabrics that help them glide quickly and smoothly through the water.

A swimmer's gear is designed to help the swimmer glide through the water as quickly as possible.

Caps cover their hair. Goggles help the swimmers see clearly and protect their eyes from pool chemicals. Coaches work with young athletes to teach them all the strokes and skills.

At the Meet

Swimmers use four basic strokes, or movements, in national and international competitions. These are the crawl, the backstroke, the breaststroke, and the butterfly stroke.

The crawl, the fastest stroke, was invented in Australia and popularized by U.S. Olympic

swimmer Johnny Weissmuller in the 1920s. Using this stroke, Weissmuller became the first man to swim the 100-meter freestyle in under

Johnny Weissmuller doing the crawl

60 seconds. He won five gold medals in the 1924 and 1928 Olympic Games.

The hardest stroke is the butterfly stroke, sometimes called "the dolphin." The swimmer's arms move forward and back like

The butterfly stroke

a butterfly's wings. At the same time, both legs kick up and down in unison, like a dolphin's tail. It takes a tremendous amount of energy and strength to do the butterfly correctly.

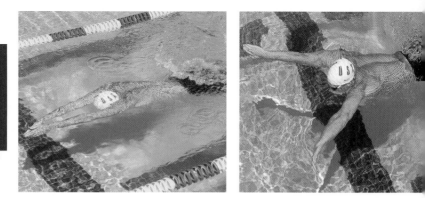

A sequence of photos showing the breaststroke

A single swimming competition includes many different races. Men and women compete separately. The races are organized into groups according to the four basic strokes. In the "freestyle" category, a swimmer can use any stroke. Of course, swimmers almost always choose the crawl—the fastest stroke.

Each category includes several races of different distances. For instance, there is the 100-meter breaststroke and the 200-meter breaststroke, the 200-meter freestyle and the 400-meter freestyle. The shortest race at a swim meet is the 50-meter freestyle. The longest race is 800 meters for women, 1,500 meters for

A freestyle race (left)
and a relay race (above)

men. In addition to individual races there are also team competitions—relay races.

Officials watch the races closely to make sure that every swimmer competes fairly.

Stroke judges see that each competitor uses the proper stroke for the race. Turn judges check to see if the swimmers go all the way to the end and touch the pool wall before turning for the next lap.

Turn judges make sure the swimmers touch the end of the pool before turning for the next lap.

The pool and time
clock at the 1983
Pan Am Games

A time clock measures speed to the nearest 100th of a second. In the end, the fastest swimmer wins.

Most swimmers are better at one stroke than another. Some have quick bursts of power and speed that help them do well in short races. Others have the steady strength and stamina to win the long races.

Only a few swimmers excel in every category. American Mark Spitz is one of them.

Mark Spitz is considered one of the greatest swimmers of all time.

During his incredible career, Spitz earned eleven Olympic medals—seven of them gold! He is known as one of the greatest swimmers of all time.

Synchronized Swimming

Synchronized swimming

Esther Williams in Million Dollar Mermaid

Synchronized swimming is a water sport that combines grace and rhythm with acrobatic skills. The swimmers synchronize—or match—their movements to music. They use different strokes to create patterns and figures in the water. There are solo, duet, and team competitions.

Years ago, synchronized swimming was called "water ballet." The sport became extremely popular in the 1950s, when Esther Williams performed dazzling routines in movies like *Million Dollar Mermaid*. Synchronized swimming became an official Olympic sport in 1984.

Diving

Diving is one of the most exciting—and dangerous—sports. A diver leaps from a platform or a springboard into a special pool called a diving pit. The diving pit is usually 16 feet (5 m) deep. While in the air, the diver performs various flips, twists, and somersaults.

A straight reverse dive (left) and a somersault during a dive (above)

It takes grace and strength to be a good diver. It also takes courage. If a mistake is made in the jump, the diver may hit the water in the wrong position—such as flat on the back or stomach. It would be just as painful as landing on a concrete sidewalk! A bad dive can cause life-threatening injuries, including a broken neck.

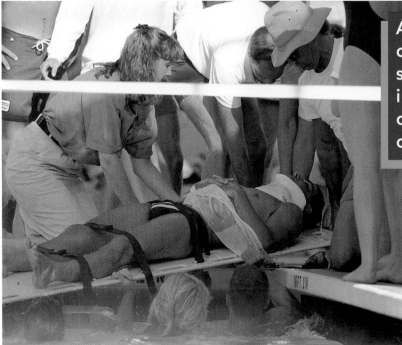

A bad dive can cause serious injury to one's back or neck.

A "clean" entry

Skillful divers make sure their hands or feet enter the water first. This breaks the surface of the water and softens the impact. If a diver enters the water correctly, there is hardly any splash. This is called a "clean" entry.

Divers sometimes use a special harness outside the pool to help them perfect their moves.

Most competitive divers work with coaches who teach them the proper techniques. Many divers use a trampoline to help them practice their jumps. Others take gymnastics training to develop their strength and flexibility. Like all athletes, divers must be sure to eat healthy foods and get plenty of rest.

The Diving Competition

There are two kinds of competitive diving—springboard diving and platform diving. As in swimming competitions, men and women divers compete separately.

A springboard measures 16 feet (5 m) long and 20 inches (51 cm) wide. The board

The flexibility of a springboard gives a diver extra height during the dive.

may be as high as 10 feet (3 m) above the water. A springboard is thin and flexible so that a diver can bounce on the board as he or she begins the dive.

A platform board is longer than a springboard, and much higher above the water. The length of the board is 20 feet (6 m); the height, 16.4 feet (5 m), 24.6 feet (7.5 m), or 33 feet (10 m).

A backward dive (far left), a reverse (left) and a twist (below)

In a competition, a diver must perform a series of dives from each of several different dive groups. The names of these groups describe the diver's position. The springboard diving groups are forward, backward, reverse, inward, and twist.

Platform diving includes these five groups and adds a sixth— the armstand group. For this group, the diver jumps from a handstand position.

In competition, divers perform both "required" dives and "optionals." For an optional dive, the competitor may choose from more than eighty acceptable

The straight position (left),
the tuck position (middle),
and the pike position (right)

types of dives. Each dive
includes different movements or
skills, ranging from very simple
to extremely difficult.

All diving moves originate
from one of three basic body
positions: straight, tuck, or pike.
In a tuck, the knees are bent
and the head and body curl

around the legs—like a cannonball. In the pike position, the body is bent forward from the waist toward the legs. The legs must be straight, with toes pointed.

A panel of judges awards points for each dive. The judges watch a diver's takeoff, midair routine, and entry into the water. They give points for good form and technique. Divers earn extra points for difficult moves. They lose

Judges watching a dive

points for sloppy movements or mistakes. A dive is scored on a scale of 0 to 10. All the scores for each dive are added together for a total score.

Just like swimming, diving requires strength and skill.

Golden Boy

Greg Louganis is known as one of the greatest divers in the history of the sport. He competed in three Olympics— 1976, 1984, and 1988.

Louganis became the first man to score more than 700 points for 11 dives—receiving a perfect "10" from each one of the judges. He won a total of five Olympic medals in his career, including four gold and one silver.

Chinese Olympic diving champion Fu Mingxia

Athletes in both sports make the commitment to spend hours practicing each day. In competition, the pressure can be intense. It's a challenge for anyone. But as the winners will tell you, the thrill of victory makes it all worthwhile.

To Find Out More

Here are some additional resources to help you learn more about swimming and diving:

 **Books**

Rouse, Jeff. **The Young Swimmer.** DK Publishing, Inc., 1997.

Sandelson, Robert. **Swimming and Diving.** Macmillan Publishing Company, 1991.

Verrier, John. **Swimming and Diving.** Heineman Library, 1996.

Verrier, John. **Swimming.** Heineman Library, 1997.

Organizations and Online Sites

Federation Internationale de Natation Amateur (FINA)
Ave de Beaumont 9
Rez-de-Chausee
1012 Lausanne, Switzerland

This is the international federation for swimmng and diving.

United States Diving, Inc.
Pan American Plaza,
Suite 430
201 South Capitol Ave,
Indianapolis, IN 46225
http://www.usdiving.org

This is recognized as the national governing body of the sport of diving in the United States.

USA Swimming KidPool
http://www.usswim.org/kidpool/

This kids' section of the USA Swimming website includes an email exchange to meet other kids interested in swimming, a forum for exchanging ideas about swimming, a photo gallery of famous swimmers, and much more.

United States Olympic Committee (USOC)
Olympic House
One Olympic Plaza
Colorado Springs, CO
80909-5760
http://www.usoc.org

The United States Olympic Committee supervises Olympic activity for the United States. Its website includes everything you'd want to know about Olympic sports, past and present.

Important Words

asthma illness that affects the lungs and makes breathing difficult

backward dive diver begins on the end of the board with back to the water, then rotates the body away from the board

determination firm or fixed purpose

inward dive diver begins on the end of the board with back to the water, then rotates the body toward the board

popularized made popular or familiar

relay race in which each member of a team races a certain distance and is then replaced by a teammate

reverse dive diver faces the front of the board, then rotates the body toward the board

stamina the ability to keep on doing a challenging physical activity

synchronize to match exactly

Index

Meet the Author

Christin Ditchfield is the author of several books for Children's Press, including five True Books on Summer Olympic sports. Her interviews with celebrity athletes have appeared in magazines all over the world. Ms. Ditchfield makes her home in Sarasota, Florida.

Photographs ©: AllSport USA: 4, 23 (Al Bello), 29 left (Denis Boulanger/Agence Vandystadt), 38 (Phil Cole), 30 (Tim DeFrisco), 22 right, 32, 42 bottom (Tony Duffy), 37 bottom right (Jed Jacobsohn), 37 left (Bob Martin), 41 (Mike Powell), 27 top (Pascal Rondeau), 36 (Jamie Squire), 14 (Todd Warshaw), 42 top; AP/Wide World Photos: 43 (Amy Sancetta); Archive Photos: 8 (Yannis Behrakis/Reuters), 18 (Popperfoto), 12 (Ben Schnall), 27 bottom; David Madison Sports Images: cover, 7, 20, 21, 22 left, 24, 29 right, 31, 35, 37 top right, 39 center; Liaison Agency, Inc.: 11 top, 26 (Hulton Getty), 17 (Sam Sargent); Network Aspen: 15 (John Russell); Tony Stone Images: 39 left (Lori Adamski Peek), 2 (Mike Hewitt), 39 right (Dimitri Iundt), 1 (David Madison), 11 bottom, 27 center (Dennis O'Clair), 19 (Alan Thornton).